STRONG IN THE LORD

CTA
His Message. Your Mission.

A. Trevor Sutton

The mission of CTA is
to glorify God by providing purposeful products
that lift up and encourage the body of Christ—
because we love him!

STRONG IN THE LORD®

Devotions for Men

by A. Trevor Sutton

http://atrevorsutton.com

Copyright © 2016 CTA, Inc.
1625 Larkin Williams Rd.
Fenton, MO 63026

www.CTAinc.com

978-1-940088-88-4

PRINTED IN THAILAND

WEEK ONE

Stronger than Fear

Fear was a constant companion for David. Wild animals, war, and worry gave him plenty of fearful moments. Yet, the strength of the Lord always proved to be stronger than David's fear.

Fear may be a constant companion for you, too. Financial fiascos, family disruptions, and an uncertain future can give you plenty of fearful moments. Still, the strength of the Lord will always prove to be stronger than any fear you can experience.

PAW, CLAW, AND GOLIATH

David said, "The LORD who delivered me from the paw of the lion and from the paw of the bear will deliver me from the hand of this Philistine." And Saul said to David, "Go, and the LORD be with you!"

1 Samuel 17:37

Goliath was scary. Lions are scarier. Goliath had five fingers; lions have five retractable claws. Goliath's voice could be heard a mile away; a lion's roar echoes over five miles. Goliath could not sprint for any meaningful distance; lions capture their prey at fifty miles per hour.

David fought hand-to-claw combat with a lion. David then went hand-to-claw with a bear. As a shepherd, David had to confront the predators circling his flock.

So when the time came to confront the predators circling his people, David knew what to do: be strong in the Lord! God had delivered David from the paw of a predator; God would deliver him from the ginormous hand of the Philistine predator named Goliath. The Lord had already shown he was stronger than a lion. There was no reason to think that a lesser foe—Goliath—would prove too strong for God.

In Christ Jesus, God has shown that he is stronger than any predator circling you today:

- Jesus has proven his strength over disease by many miraculous healings.
- He has demonstrated his power over nature by settling storms.

He has overpowered even death itself by leaving his own tomb empty on Resurrection morning.

Jesus is stronger than any foe. On the cross, Jesus went hand-to-nail against death. Even when the giant weight of sin lay on his shoulders, Jesus remained victorious. Even when his life lay in the claw of hell, Jesus prevailed.

Despite the many predators that may be hungrily encircling you and your family today—trial and temptation, fatigue and fear, stress and suffering—God will prevail. When it comes time to confront those predators, you know what to do: be strong in the Lord. He is stronger.

God will give you his strength when the paw of fear pushes against you. The Lord will strengthen you when the claw of any enemy digs into your family. You are stronger than any foe in the strength of Christ Jesus.

Prayer starter: Lord Jesus, fortify me with your strength as I confront the predators . . .

A HUMAN DARTBOARD

Saul hurled the spear, for he thought, "I will pin David to the wall." But David evaded him twice.

1 Samuel 18:11

Lawn darts combine two great pastimes: lawn games and darts. The object of the game is to throw large darts across the yard and land them within a circular target. Every dart thrown within the target is worth one point, and the first person to twenty-one points wins.

There is, however, an unwritten rule in lawn darts: everyone still alive at the end of the game wins. Many countries have banned the game because it has caused so many accidental injuries; the sharp tip on the end of the massive darts is a threat even to careful contestants.

Scripture tells us that Saul played human darts with David. Jealousy and hatred prompted Saul to hurl his spear at David in an attempt to kill him. This was no accident; this was an outright assassination attempt.

Being a human dartboard is a fearful occupation. Spears whizzing past your head can cause more than a little anxiety! David had no need for fear, however, because God was with him. Instead, . . .

Saul was afraid of David because the LORD was with him but had departed from Saul.

1 Samuel 18:12

Do you ever feel like you have a target painted on your chest? Unpaid bills spilling out of the mailbox can sting like darts in the flesh. Piles of unfinished projects at work can feel like spear tips jabbing into your side.

roken relationships, battered health, and personal failures ying in your direction can make you feel like a human artboard.

n times like that, remember: God's strength is stronger than ny problem life can throw at you. Your Lord is with you. lis strength is your strength. Christ Jesus, God in human esh, absorbed every dart of guilt and shame as he hung on the cross—even the dart of death. Jesus took the nails or you.

Now, by faith in him, your guilt is gone. The many darts that fe throws at you may hurt; yet, you can live without fear, urning to Christ for protection and peace.

Prayer starter: Lord, when Satan's temptations descend on me like a cloud of darts, remind me they cannot stick . . .

STONEWALL COURAGE

Blessed be the LORD, my rock, who trains my hands for war, and my fingers for battle; he is my steadfast love and my fortress, my stronghold and my deliverer.

Psalm 144:1–2

His full, given name was Thomas Jonathan Jackson. However, most of us know him instead as Stonewall Jackson, a lieutenant general in the American Civil War. He earned his name and his reputation on the battlefield; while everyone else trembled in their boots, he stood firm, courageous, like a stone wall.

Stonewall Jackson's determination in battle was second only to his determination in prayer. He prayed before and after each battle. He prayed for the cadets under his leadership and for the soldiers wounded in battle. His courage came, not from his own determination or even from his prayers, but from the God to whom he prayed.

Long before Stonewall Jackson, David had a reputation for stalwart courage. While others trembled in their sandals, he stood firm with unyielding resolve. The Philistines and Moabites could not shake him; the might of their chariots and warriors did not slow him down.

Prayer fueled David's battlefield courage. He prayed before and after he led God's people into combat. He prayed in defeat and in victory. David's courage came, not from his own determination, but from the God to whom he prayed. He relied on the strength only the Lord could provide.

Christ Jesus lived a life of courage like no other. Some have the courage to die for their country; Jesus courageously died for you and for me. Some face enemy armies despite overwhelming odds; Jesus faced all the hosts of evil and of death itself—in love for us.

Your many responsibilities demand rock-solid courage, too. Your family may look to you as their stonewall protector. You may have children who need you to model for them God's protecting care. Your job may require you to stand strong in the face of opposition or temptation.

Only as your Lord strengthens you will you have the courage you need to face each new day. True and lasting courage comes from Christ Jesus, the source of all strength.

Prayer starter: Fill me, O Lord Jesus, with your strength. Give me unshakable courage as I fulfill my many responsibilities, relying on you . . .

THE FLAG OF LIFE

Saul sought to pin David to the wall with the spear, but he eluded Saul, so that he struck the spear into the wall. And David fled and escaped that night.

1 Samuel 19:10

Capture the Flag is a favorite children's game. The game is wonderfully simple: two teams, two flags, and tons of running. Although children often play this game, it did not originate on a lazy afternoon during the days of summer vacation.

Capture the Flag traces its origins to the battlefield. In battle, capturing an opponent's flag requires both the guts to enter enemy territory and the ability to make a fleet-footed escape immediately thereafter. For centuries, when soldiers saw their enemy's flag captured or lowered, they knew the battle was essentially over.

God had anointed David as king of Israel and had promised David he would one day "capture the flag" from Saul; David would replace the disobedient Saul as king. Strengthened by God's promise, David was gutsy enough to serve in Saul's camp.

David was also wise enough to know when it was time to make a fleet-footed escape. David ran away from death to ensure he would one day see God's promise come true.

Jesus, on the other hand, ran toward death to fulfill God's promises to rescue us from Satan. David dodged spears. Jesus did not dodge; a Roman spear pierced his heart. In dying, Christ seized the victory over death. Now, sin, Satan, and death are vanquished. Today, our Savior rules in our lives for our good.

till today, though, the church of Christ is engaged in a mop-up operation on the field of battle. You reside in enemy territory. Evil surrounds you. You fight skirmishes every day. Though Jesus has captured the flag of life, Satan's spears are still aimed at you. Temptations still threaten. Struggles and hardships still chase after you.

Jesus is your place of safety. You can run to him from Satan's arrows. In every temptation, he will strengthen you. In every time of guilt, he will forgive you. In every trouble, he will defend you. And in death, he will share his victory with you.

Prayer starter: Christ Jesus, give me fleet-footed escape from the evil surrounding me. Let me flee to you in full confidence . . .

THE FEAR FACTOR?

God is my strength and power.

2 Samuel 22:33 KJV

Were you a *Fear Factor* fan? In this once-popular television program contestants faced dizzying heights, creepy creatures, and dark depths. Competitors jumped from airplanes, ate bugs, and swam with sharks. Snakes, scorpions, and disgusting slime were standard challenges.

Confronting fear after fear caused many contestants to drop out. If the tank of leeches did not make them quit, the tightrope walk between two multi-story buildings ofte would. As the contest ended, the one fearless person left standing would hear the program host repeat these words: "Evidently, fear is not a factor for you."

Dangers abound in daily life. There is no need to seek out recreational fear, no need to eat bugs, no need to maneuver sports cars under the flatbed of a semitrailer. Daily life provides more than enough fear-provoking situations. Will there be anything left in the checking account at the end of the month? Will I outlive my savings in retirement? Is this twinge in my chest anything to worry about? Can Homeland Security prevent the next terrorist attack? No, there's no need to look for fear. Fear will find you soon enough.

Despite life's dangers, fear need not be a factor for the people of God. As Jesus lived here on earth, he filled empty bellies and proved himself strong over scarcity. He healed broken bodies and calmed troubled souls. He forgave sins and kept his promises to make all things new. Jesus ventured even into the dark depths of death, returning in triumph over the grave:

he sting of death is sin, and the power of sin is the law.
ut thanks be to God, who gives us the victory through
ur Lord Jesus Christ.

1 Corinthians 15:56–57

our Lord is stronger than any fear, stronger than any
vorry that has been keeping you up at night. Debt?
isease? Death? All are flimsy foes when compared to
ne strength of the Lord. Sickness? Suffering? Sorrow?
hese have nothing on you when you are fortified by
our Savior and his unshakable promises.

Prayer starter: My strong Lord, keep me from letting fear be a factor as I serve you. When I am filled with fear, remind me of your strength . . .

SUNDAY

David was one of many men in the Bible to face his fear in the strength of the Lord. In every age, God's people can be strong—strong in the Lord:

Do not be frightened, and do not be dismayed, for the LORD your God is with you wherever you go.

Joshua 1:9

The LORD is good, a stronghold in the day of trouble; he knows those who take refuge in him.

Nahum 1:7

Be strong in the Lord and in the strength of his might.

Ephesians 6:10

You are certainly not the only one to be overwhelmed by fear at times. You certainly need not be one who faces fear alone. Call on your Lord's strength! He will hear and help!

WEEK TWO

Stronger than Failure

Failure always stings—
minor mistakes and major
meltdowns alike. David often
succeeded—at failing! Still,
God's forgiveness proved
always stronger than
David's failures.

Do you ever feel that you
are succeeding at failure?
Forgetting your mom's
birthday? Not quite
landing that important
account? Hurting someone
in your family?

Then remember: You are more
than the sum total of your
failures. In the cross, your Lord
forgives, and he provides the
strength you need to keep
moving forward. You are
strong—in the Lord!

TUB OF TEMPTATION

It happened, late one afternoon, when David arose from his couch and was walking on the roof of the king's house, that he saw from the roof a woman bathing; and the woman was very beautiful.

2 Samuel 11:2

Stub your toe against the wall and it will hurt. Do it again, and it will hurt again. No matter how many times you do it the outcome is always the same: pain.

Dip a toe into temptation and you will regret it. Do it again and you will regret it again. No matter how many times you deliberately walk into temptation, the outcome is always the same: pain and guilt.

David thought he could peek at Bathsheba without consequences; he tried to dip a toe into the waters of temptation without falling into a tub of sin. He was wrong. A trickle of lust turned into a flood of adultery. Then the cover-ups began. One sin led to another until a cascade of guilt and shame began to overflow from David's life.

It took months before David finally came to repentance. When he did, he prayed:

Wash me thoroughly from my iniquity, and cleanse me from my sin! Psalm 51:2

God did forgive David, washing away David's sin because of the sacrifice Jesus would one day make on Calvary's cross. Jesus was David's substitute, and he is yours, too.

Christ Jesus obeyed when we have not. He faced a steady stream of temptations throughout his life here on earth, and he resisted them all:

In the wilderness, Satan tempted Jesus to prioritize his own needs rather than the Father's plan to rescue us. In the Garden of Gethsemane, Satan tempted Jesus to abandon the Father's will for our salvation.
On Calvary, Satan tempted Jesus to come down from the cross, seizing power and fame, rather than earning our pardon.

:sus rejected every temptation. He obeyed his heavenly ther fully in every respect, living and dying for you.

ow, when you are tempted, you need not rely on your wn power, but on Christ's strength. Together with the ostle Paul you can say:

ierefore I will boast all the more gladly of my 'eaknesses, so that the power of Christ may rest >on me. 2 Corinthians 12:9

Prayer starter: Sinless Jesus, when temptations surround me . . .

THE BALM OF SALVATION

The thing that David had done displeased the LORD.

2 Samuel 11:27

Tree trimming poses many dangers. Falling off a ladder ca break bones and bruise brains. Misjudge the angle of a cu and you may drop a tree right through your roof. Slip wi the chainsaw, and you will end up in the emergency roor

Poison ivy is not the most obvious hazard to tree trimmer But it can cause immense agony. Touch the plant but onc and you have the oil on your skin. Touch that oil, and it spreads. No alarms go off immediately; it takes time for th toxic oil to do its work. But in a few hours, prickly sores and bubbling boils can cover your whole body.

David's sin with Bathsheba spread like poison ivy. The init touch of lust set off no immediate alarms; sin's toxic pow is seldom evident right away. But as the hours and days ticked by, sin's lethal effects began. Prickly shame and the pus-filled bubbles of moral failure soon scarred David's soul.

That's the point at which he tried to find relief using a swab of lies:

In the morning David wrote a letter to Joab and sent i by the hand of Uriah. In the letter he wrote, "Set Uriah in the forefront of the hardest fighting, and then draw back from him, that he may be struck down, and die."

2 Samuel 11:14–15

The only remedy for poison ivy is its removal. Removal was the only remedy for David's sin, too. Covering the festering guilt with lies and murder would not heal the wounds. Only God's soothing mercy could do that.

o, in mercy, God sent the prophet Nathan to confront
David with his guilt and lead him to true repentance. David
confessed his sins, and in grace, God forgave.

Even today, the strong, healing balm of Jesus' pardon is the
only cure for sin. Through his death and resurrection, he
removes your guilt. When you are tempted to cover your
wrongdoing with excuses, stop! When you are tempted to
conceal or camouflage your failures, stop! Instead, ask your
Savior to forgive your guilt before sin spreads, before it
causes further damage.

Prayer starter: Healing Lord, when the toxic oil of sin contaminates me, remind me to come to you for help . . .

WHEN LEADERS FAIL

Now therefore arise, go out and speak kindly to your servants, for I swear by the LORD, if you do not go, not a man will stay with you this night, and this will be worse for you than all the evil that has come upon you from your youth until now.

2 Samuel 19:7

History deems the Battle of Stirling Bridge in 1297 a crucial moment in the First War of Scottish Independence. The Scots occupied ground on the north bank of the River Forth. To engage them, the English could either ford the shallow river upstream or cross it on the Stirling Bridge. Fording would be long and hard. Crossing the bridge would be quick and easy. But there was a catch: the narrow bridge would allow only two cavalrymen to cross at a time.

Pressured by the king's representative to save time and money, the Earl of Surrey ordered the English troops across the narrow bridge. This decision would be his undoing.

From nearby high ground, Scottish archers watched as a vanguard of English crossed the bridge. When the Scots saw that a significant—but manageable—number had crossed, they released a swarm of arrows and swooped down with spears. Bunched up at the bridgehead, the horsemen had no escape route. The remaining English troops, trapped on the south bank of the river, watched the slaughter unfold, helpless to prevent it.

His confidence gone, the Earl of Surrey ordered Stirling Bridge destroyed, and then he retreated. It was an epic leadership failure.

ng David created his own epic leadership failure. Civil war divided the kingdom between David and his son Absalom. The two armies fought relentlessly. David's troops eventually prevailed and Absalom died in battle. Despite Absalom's obvious treason, David mourned uncontrollably for him.

David's grief shamed his troops. They had defeated the traitorous Absalom. He would not create chaos again. Wasn't that a good thing? Joab, David's general, confronted the king. "Thank your troops for their loyalty," he urged, "or you will have a rebellion worse than Absalom's on your hands." Thankfully, David listened.

Human leaders fail. Our divine leader, Christ Jesus, never does. Instead, our Commander forgives our failures. You miscalculate, miscommunicate, make mistakes; Jesus makes all things new.

Prayer starter: O Lord, your leadership is perfect! Make me new day by day. As I lead, teach me to rely on your wisdom and strength . . .

MORE THAN ENOUGH

David's heart struck him after he had numbered the people. And David said to the LORD, "I have sinned greatly in what I have done. But now, O LORD, please take away the iniquity of your servant, for I have done very foolishly."   2 Samuel 24:10

Rapscallion, a word found in many dictionaries, refers to a mischievous person. *Knavery*, a word also found in many dictionaries, describes mischievous behavior. You could say that rapscallions love knavery.

Dictionaries teem with great words. Some of those words are common; others are obsolete. The word *enough* falls into the common category. You can find it in almost every English dictionary, even dictionaries for children. With only two syllables and six letters, it is a simple word.

Look through the sinful human heart, however, and the word *enough* is strangely missing. We never have enough. We always want more—more possessions, more time, more experiences, and more power.

David didn't think he had enough. He wanted more people so he could parlay them into more power and more prosperity. More people would produce more taxable goods and services. More people meant more young men able to serve in David's army.

The Lord had already given David far more than he could have once imagined. Yet David ordered his commanders to take a census. The order was knavery, driven by greed and pride. Joab, David's trusted advisor, even told David he was being a rapscallion. But David went ahead anyway because he did not have enough.

efore long, God moved David to see the foolishness of vanting more. David realized his failure as a leader. He realized that God's grace is more than enough.

hrist Jesus gives you more than enough. His grace is more han enough to meet all your needs. Are you tempted to hink you need more time? Then remember, all eternity is ours in Christ. Are you tempted to think you need more ossessions? Then remember, all the riches of heaven are ours. They are your inheritance through faith in Christ. re you tempted to want more power? Then remember, hrist's strength is yours, just for the asking.

Prayer starter: Generous God, you have given me more than enough in Christ Jesus. Open my eyes to see the bounty of your great goodness . . .

GREATER THAN A THOUSAND FAILURES

God is my strength and power.

2 Samuel 22:33 KJV

"How does it feel to fail so many times?" A reporter once asked Thomas Edison that question about his many failed experiments. Edison had experimented with thousands of different materials in an attempt to find the best filament for the lightbulb. And all the experiments failed.

Edison supposedly responded to the reporter's question: "I have not failed. I've just found 1,000 ways that won't work." Edison was not willing to let a few failed experiments (or even a few thousand failed experiments!) stop him. By turning his failures into opportunities to learn, Edison charged on toward another invention.

Look back through the past week and count the times you have failed to keep your word. Review the past year to determine how many times you have failed in your responsibilities. If you reflect on the entirety of your life, the number of failures quickly becomes staggering. Any lifetime easily includes tens of thousands of failures.

Still, in Christ, your failures need not define you. You are not the sum total of your many mistakes. God does not count your missteps. Instead, your Lord took your failure upon himself in Christ Jesus.

On the cross, Jesus paid for your every failure, your every sin. He buried your failures in his own tomb. On the third day, Jesus emerged from that tomb, alive again, leaving your failures behind. All of them. Jesus is victorious over death. Jesus is champion over failure.

And Jesus is strong enough to turn your failures upside down. In Christ Jesus, you can speak a strong word of victory over your sins: "I am not defeated. I have simply found 10,000 reasons why I need Christ Jesus." Don't let your many mistakes demoralize you. Instead, use your failures as a reason for rejoicing in God's mercy.

Then, press on with courage. Move forward in confidence. Go without fear. Jesus has removed the sting from failure. He has declared you holy, blameless in his cross. His love, his sacrifice is stronger than any or all of your sins, any or all of your failures.

Prayer starter: Failure is something I know well, Christ Jesus. Help me turn my many mistakes into opportunities to see your mercy . . .

SUNDAY

What do you have in common with every person in the Bible? Failure. Everyone—then and now—is familiar with failure. Adam and Abraham failed. Joshua and Jonah failed. But God's strength is always stronger than any failure:

My flesh and my heart may fail, but God is the strength of my heart and my portion forever.

Psalm 73:26

The LORD within her is righteous; he does no injustice; every morning he shows forth his justice; each dawn he does not fail.

Zephaniah 3:5

Save us, we pray, O LORD! O LORD, we pray, give us success!

Psalm 118:25

Failure is forgiven in the perfect sacrifice of Jesus Christ. Jesus makes all things new. Draw strength from that good news as you continue to serve in your family, church, and community.

_____

_____

_____

_____

WEEK THREE

Stronger than Family Problems

Like a disease eating away at a once-sturdy oak, sin and its consequences ate away at David's family tree. Still, God refused to let that tree die. He had promised to send our Savior in the line of David, and he would keep that promise.

God grafted you into his family tree through faith in Christ. Although troubles still arise in your life, even family problems, you can rely on the Lord's strength as you address them.

RESTORING THE FAMILY TREE

There shall come forth a shoot from the stump of Jesse, and a branch from his roots shall bear fruit.

Isaiah 11:1

Families share in each other's blessings. One shared blanket covers the whole family as you huddle together on the couch on movie night. The rusty family station wagon gets passed down from one generation to the next. Members of the extended family from near and far share love and laughter around the holiday dinner table.

Families also share in each other's problems. A bad day for one person casts a dark cloud over the whole family. Financial woes cause stress for everyone. Anger can spread from person to person until even the dog is mad about something!

David's family knew about sharing family joys. Newborn babies. Opportunities for worship. Invasions repelled. Safety restored. The Lord gave David and his family countless reasons for rejoicing together.

But like noxious weeds, serious problems also stressed David's family tree. Many sins grew into a tangled vine of troubles. The knots and gnarls of selfishness and treachery pockmarked David's family tree.

Despite Satan's best efforts, that tree was never destroyed. Though it was eventually cut down, a shoot grew up from the stump of Jesse—David's father. Jesus Christ is that shoot, the Savior whom God had promised. The family tree of faith that sprouts from that shoot will never be destroyed.

By God's grace, you have a place of honor in Jesus' family tree. Through faith, you are the blessed and righteous tree described in Psalm 1:3:

. . planted by streams of water that yields its fruit in its season, and its leaf does not wither.

When problems grow up in and around your family like noxious weeds, remember that you have a Savior, Friend, and Brother in Christ Jesus. He knows and loves the members of your family more than you can imagine! He cares for them more deeply than you will ever know!

Draw strength from your Savior as you witness to his love despite family problems and sins. Ask him for wisdom in using every challenge as an opportunity to share Jesus' promises, especially his promise of forgiveness.

Prayer starter: O Lord, my family knows both joys and struggles. I need your strength . . .

THE BOND BETWEEN FATHER AND SON

Joab went to the king and told him, and he summoned Absalom. So he came to the king and bowed himself on his face to the ground before the king, and the king kissed Absalom.

2 Samuel 14:33

Duct tape can fix just about anything from broken brackets to fraying fabric. When duct tape won't quite do the job, then zip ties often will. Jumbled cords? Loose cables? Lock them in place with a zip tie. When duct tape and zip ties both fail, you are left with one, last option: super glue!

Yet, there is a bond even stronger than duct tape, zip ties, and super glue combined: the bond between father and son. Time, distance, and trouble cannot break this bond. (Or can they?)

David's family history records a time when the father-son bond nearly dissolved. David's son Amnon raped his half sister, Tamar. When Tamar's brother Absalom heard about it, he waited for David to act, but David never did. So Absalom put a plot in place to kill Amnon. Then, Absalom fled into self-imposed exile.

For years, David and Absalom did not see one another. Much as David loved Absalom, he could not bring himself to summon his son home again. David neither punished Absalom, nor forgave him. Absalom lived in a gray zone—a never-never land of exile—until David's general, Joab, found a way to reunite father and son once again.

At one point, the woman Joab used as a messenger remarked to David:

[The Lord] devises means so that the banished one will not remain an outcast.

2 Samuel 14:14

This observation applies to you even more clearly than it did to Absalom. Sin threatened to break the bond between you and your heavenly Father. But in Jesus, God made a way for you—one who should have been banished forever—to return home once more.

As Jesus hung on the cross, he bore the full weight of your sin. The wrath of God that should have fallen on you fell on Jesus instead. For a time on that Good Friday, Father and Son were separated, as Jesus endured the agony of hell in your place. Now, by faith in Jesus, you are reconciled to God.

Prayer starter: Lord, as you have reconciled me to yourself, help me heal broken bonds, too . . .

DAD TAUGHT ME

When Solomon was old his wives turned away his heart after other gods, and his heart was not wholly true to the LORD his God, as was the heart of David his father.

1 Kings 11:4

You must learn how to throw a football; snapping the perfect spiral is not a natural ability. You must learn how to fix a clogged drainpipe; plumbing is not an innate talent. You must learn to show respect to others; respect is not an automatic behavior. When you ask children where they learned these things, they will often say: "Dad taught me!"

You must learn to drink milk directly from the carton; it is not a natural behavior. You must learn to track filth through the house while wearing muddy boots; such conduct is not innate. You must learn to slurp soup from your bowl. Children generally see someone else doing it before they mimic the behavior themselves. When children are asked where they learned these things, they will often say: "Dad taught me!"

Solomon learned many lessons from his father. King David taught Solomon to rely on the Lord and on the Lord's strength. King David taught Solomon about godly leadership. King David taught Solomon about the value of worship. Seeing these behaviors modeled, Solomon wanted to mimic them.

But Solomon learned other things from King David, too. Solomon watched his father engage in political intrigue. Solomon observed the brokenness of a mismanaged family. Solomon witnessed his father's lust, anger, and greed. From David, Solomon learned both good habits and bad habits. Solomon could say in truth: "Dad taught me!"

Our heavenly Father has shown us his love and mercy in Christ's sacrifice on the cross. We have witnessed the strength of our Lord in Easter's empty tomb. But God does more than just teach us about love and mercy; he *gives us* his love and mercy through the sacrifice of Jesus.

You have the opportunity to teach your family many lessons. Teach your family to pray. Demonstrate a life of worship. Show what it means to rely fully on the Lord's strength. Then one day, they will be able to say: "You taught me!"

Prayer starter: Heavenly Father, teach me to know your love and mercy. Then enable me to teach those I love . . .

MULTIPLIED STRENGTH

God is my strength and power.

2 Samuel 22:33 KJV

The strongest animal on earth is . . . ?

Blue whales, elephants, and grizzly bears are standard on any list of the strongest animals in the world. Eagles, gorillas, and crocodiles are obvious contenders, too. Clydesdale horses, anaconda snakes, and Bengal tigers can execute impressive feats of strength.

On the other hand, ants, beetles, and fleas do not immediately come to mind. However, these animals actually top the charts in strength-to-weight competitions:

- Gorillas can carry objects ten times their body weight; ants can carry loads one thousand times their body weight!
- Humans can jump a distance five times their body's length; fleas can jump a distance two hundred times their body's length.

Impressive feats of strength indeed!

Life often demands strength much greater than your size. Your spouse may need you to have Clydesdale-like strength as you take the weight of worry off her shoulder. The children in your home, on your team, or in your Sunday school classroom look to you to protect them with the strength of a grizzly bear. Your work may require you, ant-like, to carry a load far greater than your apparent capacity.

...ou may buckle, but Jesus never will. When violent storms ...low in, Christ Jesus calms the winds and the waves with word. When temptations boil up, Jesus wrestles with evil nd turns down the heat. Your Lord has even rolled away ...e stone that once trapped you in death's dark tomb!

...sus is a force multiplier:

> You may be strong enough to work hard for a living; when you rely on Jesus, you can work that hard—with great joy.
> You may be strong enough to build a house; when you rely on Jesus, you can build a home and extend the eternal Kingdom of God into the lives of others.
> You may be strong enough to carry a heavy load for a few days; when you rely on Jesus, you can carry your own burdens and the concerns of others throughout a lifetime of service.

Prayer starter: Lord, so many people count on me. My own strength is not enough. Be my force multiplier! . . .

POUR OUT YOUR HEART

My heart is steadfast, O God! I will sing and make melody with all my being!

Psalm 108:1

Do you like to sing in the shower? Do you use the scrub brush to amplify your performance? You may think you are the next, best candidate for an appearance on Singing with the Celebs. You may be mistaken.

If you ask, others in your household may gently share the painful news. While you are belting out each golden oldie, the rest of the family is listening not-so-patiently for the final note. Pouring out your heart while you sing and scrub may be fun for you. For others? Maybe not so much.

When others here on earth aren't too anxious to hear you pour out your heart, your Lord Jesus always welcomes it. Whether you sing or simply speak, your Savior invites you to offer your gut-level feelings, fears, and failures to him in prayer. He never tires of hearing your prayers and praises. What's more, your heavenly Father will always hear, help, and offer you hope in Christ Jesus.

Throughout his lifetime, David poured out his gut-level feelings to God in prayer. As he wrestled with family challenges, as he celebrated victories, in times of fear and near despair, in times of overwhelming joy and thanksgiving, David prayed. He recorded many of these prayers and the Holy Spirit took special care to preserve them for us in the Bible, particularly the Book of Psalms. David also wrote these words of invitation:

Trust in him at all times, O people; pour out your heart before him; God is a refuge for us.

Psalm 62:8

till today, your Savior invites you to be real with him, to pour your heart out to him in prayer. Whether you use prayers written by others—like David's psalms—or use your own words as they well up in your heart and spill over your lips, your Lord will listen. He is your refuge.

So speak up. Sing out. Jesus is waiting, anxious to come alongside you to support, strengthen, and encourage you!

Prayer starter: Listening Lord, incline your ear to me. Hear when I call, help when I am in need, and renew my hope in Christ Jesus. Especially, right now, I . . . .

SUNDAY

Since the day Adam and Eve left Eden, spouses have argued over money. Since the time of Moses, children have refused to eat their peas. Relationship problems are nothing new:

When Joseph came to his brothers, they stripped him of his robe, the robe of many colors that he wore. And they took him and threw him into a pit.

Genesis 37:23–24

For it has been reported to me by Chloe's people that there is quarreling among you.

1 Corinthians 1:11

What causes quarrels and what causes fights among you? Is it not this, that your passions are at war within you?

James 4:1

Our Lord was not content to let us continue to hurt each other. In Jesus, he intervened in humanity's gnarled family tree. This weekend, pray about broken relationships. Ask for the hope and strength only God can provide.

_____

_____

_____

_____

Stronger than Fatigue

At many points in his life, David no doubt felt the fatigue of fear and failure gnawing deep within his bones. But when he wondered how he could go on, strength from the Lord revitalized him. The Lord's strength carried David through each new day.

Are you worn out? Wondering how to go on? Jesus is stronger than your fatigue. Let his strength replace your weakness. Take on each new day in the strength of the Lord.

REFRESHMENT FROM GOD

The king, and all the people who were with him, arrive
weary at the Jordan. And there he refreshed himself.

2 Samuel 16:14

The Appalachian Trail traverses some 2,168 miles. Hiking
it takes the better part of a year. Fatigue overtakes most
hikers; only a few, thru-hikers, are strong enough to
complete the journey.

Lugging the weight of a sleeping bag, camp stove, food,
a tent, and extra clothing from Maine to Georgia will tire
even the strongest hiker. Boots wear out, beards grow
long, and blisters burn. Backpack straps cut into the
shoulders, making each mile even more of a challenge.

Like a weary thru-hiker, King David carried a heavy
load as he fled for his life. He bore the weight of his
personal belongings on his shoulders and the weight of
personal regret on his heart. He dragged mistakes and
misgivings along with him as he fled for his life from his so
Absalom—now a traitor in command of a formidable arm

Fatigue swelled as David lost sight of Jerusalem, retreating
into the distance. Strong as he was, David was weary bo
physically and spiritually.

The Jordan River refreshed the king's weary body and
the bodies of the refugees who traveled with him. They
sat down beside its cool waters to drink and, perhaps,
to soak sore muscles. The soothing sound of the flowing
water was refreshing in and of itself.

Still, the cool waters of the Jordan River could not relieve David's spiritual fatigue. The Lord alone could remove David's load of regret, of remorse. The Lord alone could forgive David's failures and heal his brokenness. The Lord alone could refresh the depths of David's soul.

God refreshes and strengthens his people. Only he can turn fatigue into lasting fortitude. The strength he provides flows from knowing and believing that Christ Jesus has shouldered your sins, carrying them to his own cross. Now, he invites you to give him every one of your mistakes and misgivings, your regrets and remorse. In exchange, he will refresh you.

Listen! This is what Jesus says to you:

Come to me, all who labor and are heavy laden, and I will give you rest.

Matthew 11:28

Prayer starter: Lord, I want to serve you. But first, I need your rest. Take my regret and remorse . . .

JAB, JAB, JAB, RIGHT HOOK!

A messenger came to David, saying, "The hearts of the men of Israel have gone after Absalom."

2 Samuel 15:13

Jab, jab, jab, right hook: Boxers know that throwing a combination of punches is the best way to land a fight-ending blow. Repeating the same punch multiple times makes the opponent weary; throwing something different into the mix catches him off guard.

Jab, jab, jab, right hook: Life knows how to throw a knockout combination. Work throws problem after problem until you become weary; then an unpaid bill comes in the mail, catching you entirely off guard. Family problems hit you one after another, wearing you down. Then a health emergency blindsides you; you fall to the mat, seeing stars. Daily life can throw a deadly one-two punch.

King David took punch after punch from his traitorous son, Absalom. Prince Absalom persuaded people to follow him instead of David, his father and Israel's rightful king. Then, with his rebel army in tow, Absalom chased David out of Jerusalem and into the nearby hills.

Absalom even devised a plan to kill David: "I will come upon him while he is weary and discouraged and throw him into a panic, and all the people who are with him will flee. I will strike down only the king" (2 Samuel 17:2).

But just when it seemed David was down for the count, the Lord renewed David's strength. God intervened, thwarting Absalom's evil schemes. Before the knockout punch could land, the Lord blocked it. God's great strength prevailed.

Punch after punch, Jesus took a deadly combination of hits. The religious elites pummeled him with charges of false teaching. The Roman Empire struck with the charge of insurrection. Just when it seemed he was down for the count, hanging there in agony on the cross, Jesus prevailed. "It is finished!" he shouted in triumph. And your salvation was sealed.

Life will throw punch after punch, jabs and right hooks. Staggering bills. Startling health challenges. Stunning troubles. None of these can send you to the mat. Life cannot knock you out when you are strong in the Lord.

Prayer starter: Lord God, you made heaven and earth! Your strength is immeasurable. Guard me as I fend off life's punches and strengthen me as I serve and witness in your name . . .

LIFE OUT OF ORDER

The king was deeply moved and went up to the chamber over the gate and wept. And as he went, he said, "O my son Absalom, my son, my son Absalom! Would I had died instead of you, O Absalom, my son, my son!"

2 Samuel 18:33

"Loop, swoop, and pull." This pithy little saying teaches children how to tie their shoes. The first step is to create two identical loops. Then swoop those loops around one another to form the knot. Lastly, after you swoop the loops, you pull.

Swoop, loop, and pull will get you nowhere. Pulling first and looping last will not work either. Tying a shoelace relies on process; the first step must precede any other steps. Everything must occur in the right sequence.

Life is best lived in order, too. Babies drink milk before eating solid food. Walking comes before running. Grammar school comes before college. And, most of all, parents should precede their children to the grave. It is deeply unsettling when life gets out of order. Things fall apart when a parent outlives a child.

David outlived several of his children, but Absalom's death was arguably the bitterest pill of all. Despite his many conflicts with Absalom, despite Absalom's hotheaded and unwise decisions, and even despite Absalom's treason, David was still overwhelmed when he heard that his son Absalom had preceded him to the grave. From the depths of despair, David wept.

Grief is among the strongest of human emotions. When coupled with the kind of deep fatigue David was experiencing, grief has ruined lesser men. But in the end, David was not ruined. In David's weakest hour, the Lord gave David his strongest strength. God straightened David's spine and dried his tears. The Lord restored the king's resolve. Strong in the Lord, David overcame.

As Jesus hung on Calvary's cross, it looked like the point of his greatest weakness. It was, instead, the point of his greatest strength. At the cross, Jesus was meeting your greatest need: salvation from the disorder of sin.

In your weakest hour, God will give you his strongest strength. But first things first! Come to your Savior. Tell him your need. Ask him to make you strong—in him!

Prayer starter: Strong in the Lord. Make it so, Jesus! Especially . . .

STRENGTH THAT ENDURES

When David's time to die drew near, he commanded Solomon his son, saying, "I am about to go the way of all the earth. Be strong, and show yourself a man."

1 Kings 2:1–2

The human body is oddly similar to a car: the older it gets, the harder it is to start in the morning. Very much like our vehicles, we sputter and cough, clunk and clatter until everything warms up. Age takes its toll.

But age also has its benefits. The longer you own a car, the more you know about it. You know which groans are normal and which creaks are cause for concern. Insight and wisdom increase with experience.

The same goes for life. Age provides a perspective, a vantage point, impossible in youth. The haze of adolescent hopes and fears gives way, after a time, to a clearer vision of what is truly important.

As the time came for David to die, the king was far older and wiser than the shepherd boy who had tended Jesse' flocks in the hill country outside Bethlehem. King David wanted to share with Solomon, his son and the successor to his throne, some of the wisdom he had gained in shepherding God's people over a lifetime.

He called Prince Solomon to his bedside and began with these important words: "Be strong!" David had learned from a lifetime of experience that human strength will always fail, but the strength of the Lord, will always prevail. Muscles eventually atrophy. Bones grow frail. Human insight will disappoint. But always, the Lord remains faithful.

Are you strong in the Lord? No matter where you stand along life's path today, at some point in the future age will fatigue your bones. Stress will fatigue your mind. Work will fatigue your muscles. Life will fatigue your faith. Strength in the Lord is your only option.

For forty days in the wilderness, Christ Jesus stood toe to toe with Satan—and emerged victorious over temptation. For hour after miserable hour, Christ Jesus hung on your cross, enduring the punishment for your sins—and emerged victorious from his tomb three days later.

When you are strong in the Lord, you are ready for any challenge.

Prayer starter: Lord, fortify my mind and body, heart and soul . . .

EMPTY TO FULL

God is my strength and power.

2 Samuel 22:33 KJV

E is for empty. It is a hollow feeling. An empty gas tank will get you nowhere. Armies never march far on empty stomachs. When you are running on empty, spiritually speaking, even insignificant obstacles will pose major challenges.

F is for full. It is a surging feeling. A full gas tank sends you charging down the road behind eight strong pistons. Armies fueled by full stomachs can march miles at double time. When you are fully fueled, spiritually speaking, even major obstacles pose few challenges.

How fast can you go from full to empty? One stressful meeting can run you dry. One marathon week of work can leave you spiritually drained. One episode of extended suffering can leave you desolate and depleted.

A sapped soul is vulnerable to attack. A shattered spirit will drag you down as you lead a family, a class, a team, a troop. Try muddling along on E, and you will not get very far. Try powering through a challenging week when you are spiritually empty, and you will fail.

You need a reliable source of power, a source of strength outside yourself, an unlimited source of energy that is available whenever you need to draw from it. David came to this realization, and based on it, he wrote these words of praise:

God is my strength and power.

2 Samuel 22:33 KJV

he Lord is your strength and power, just as he was
avid's. There's no need to be running on empty. Ask your
avior to fill your heart, to top off your spirit.

e will do that as he reminds you that he has removed
ie burden of your sin. He will do that as he reminds you
iat he died your death and has, in exchange, given you
ternal life. He will do that as he draws you ever deeper
ito his Word, renewing your strength and making you to
ar on the winds of his grace.

trong in the Lord, you can live life to the fullest. Strong in
ie Lord, you can lead, counsel, and encourage others.

Prayer starter: Christ Jesus, you are the source of all strength and power. Renew my faith and teach me to live strong in the Lord. . . .

SUNDAY

Three cups of coffee later, you are still tired. Two days on the weekend are never enough time to recover from a trying week. One depleted body and soul cries out for the strength only Jesus can give. Scripture has plenty to say about fatigue:

They who wait for the LORD shall renew their strength; they shall mount up with wings like eagles; they shall run and not be weary; they shall walk and not faint.

Isaiah 40:31

If I must boast, I will boast of the things that show my weakness.

2 Corinthians 11:30

Come to me, all who labor and are heavy laden, and I will give you rest.

Matthew 11:28

For this I toil, struggling with all his energy that he powerfully works within me.

Colossians 1:29

Be strong—in the Lord!

WEEK FIVE

Strong in Faith

When David failed, he fell to his knees, asking for God's forgiveness. When he enjoyed great success, he filled the air with joyful praises. At life's end David died, relying on the Messiah, the coming Savior. Faith was David's default position.

Just as the Lord strengthened David, he wants to make you strong in faith, too. He promises to forgive your sins and fix your brokenness. By faith in Jesus, you are strong in the Lord.

STRENGTH IN THE MORNING

Let me hear in the morning of your steadfast love, for in you I trust. Make me know the way I should go, for to you I lift up my soul.

Psalm 143:8

Buzz! Buzz! Buzz! Few sounds are more annoying than the shrill screech of the alarm clock. One moment you dream of waves rolling onto the sands of a tropical beach; the next moment you are fumbling around a dark, cold room looking for the light switch. One moment, you are watching a warm sun spill out across the surf. The next, you are spilling coffee beans across the kitchen floor.

Few people would nominate the alarm clock as their favorite household appliance, even if it is the harbinger of another new day, a gift from God.

David wrote Psalm 143 as a morning prayer. He asks this of the Lord as he awakens: "Let me hear in the morning of your steadfast love, for in you I trust." Rather than cursing the alarm clock, David praised the Lord. He did not begin his day in surly sadness; he began, instead, in faith. He began by invoking the Lord's unchanging love. That unshakable love made David strong in the Lord.

Christ is your strength in the morning. Christ is your strength in the evening. At every hour, day or night, Christ Jesus gives you his strength. He is Lord of heaven and earth—and everything in between. The apostle Paul writes:

God has highly exalted him and bestowed on him the name that is above every name, so that at the name of Jesus every knee should bow, in heaven and on earth

nd under the earth, and every tongue confess that
esus Christ is Lord, to the glory of God the Father.

Philippians 2:9–11

Vhen that alarm clock goes off, you need not press the
nooze button on life. You need not roll over, pretending
our obligations will go away. Instead, you can welcome
he day, strong in the Lord. You can lift up your soul to
our Savior, trusting him to show you the path he would
ave you travel, the service he has set aside just for you.

Prayer starter: Lord, grant me your strength to take on the new day you have planned for me . . .

REMOVED AND COVERED

Blessed is the one whose transgression is forgiven, whose sin is covered. Blessed is the man against whom the LORD counts no iniquity, and in whose spirit there is no deceit.   Psalm 32:1–2

"Just slap some paint on it!" Auto body experts know that this is horrible advice. Deep scratches will not simply go away when hidden beneath a thin coat of paint. Dents and dings are never resolved by adding a layer of clear coat. Rust will continue to fester, hidden from sight.

If you want to stop the damage, you must remove the dent and only then, apply paint. Fill in the scratch, or else it will never look right. Cut out the rust and replace it with new metal. When the underlying damage is gone, then you can safely "slap some paint on it."

Like rust, sin festers. It consumes the body (and the soul). Cover-ups only seem to work, and even then, only temporarily. Sin must be forgiven, removed. Then, and only then, can it be safely covered.

When David realized the far-reaching damage his sins had caused, he saw at once that applying a clear coat of excuses would not do. Instead, he threw himself on God's mercy.

When sin scrapes your heart, dents your relationships, and scuffs up your life, Christ is strong to help. He will cut out the impurity, replacing it with his own righteousness. He will grind away the covetousness, replacing it with contentment. He will fill every gap and hole with his very own righteousness.

e will not stop until he has completely restored you and stored in you the joy of his salvation.

hese are not cheap repairs:

ou were ransomed from the futile ways inherited from our forefathers, not with perishable things such as lver or gold, but with the precious blood of Christ.

1 Peter 1:18–19

low that Jesus has done all this for you, be strong in the ord. Flee from sin. Refuse to let it dent, scrape, and scuff our life. Take full advantage of God's powerful Word as ou battle on:

ut to death therefore what is earthly in you: exual immorality, impurity, passion, evil desire, and ovetousness, which is idolatry.

Colossians 3:5

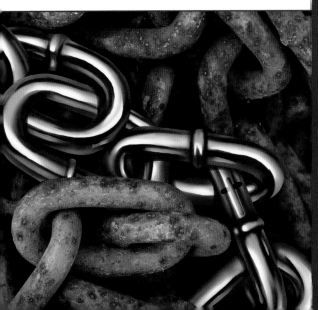

HATE SIN AND LOVE FORGIVENESS

Have mercy on me, O God, according to your steadfast love; according to your abundant mercy blot out my transgressions.   Psalm 51:1

Carpenters know how to use a template. Measure, calculate, and measure again. When every measurement is perfect, then it is time to cut the first board. The template becomes the standard for all the other boards. Rather than measuring each board individually, the template makes it possible to cut hundreds of perfect pieces.

Our Lord, divine Carpenter of the universe, is the standard of all holiness. He is the benchmark for perfect love. His perfect justice is the norm to which our ideas of justice are to conform. His divine mercy is the ideal for all human mercy.

God measured, calculated, and formed the heart of David following the template of his own heart. Scripture tells us what the Lord had in mind:

He raised up David to be their king, of whom he testified and said, "I have found in David the son of Jesse a man after my heart, who will do all my will."
                                    Acts 13:22

David was a man after God's own heart. David's *heart*, however, was clearly broken. The Lord did not fail, but David did. David's heart was inclined to sin.

Lust drove David to sleep with Bathsheba. Deceit motivated David to kill Uriah. War stained David's heart and David's hands.

God does not have a heart for any of these things. God loves mercy, justice, and peace. How could the Lord possibly call David "a man after his own heart"?

Sin and forgiveness connected the heart of God and the heart of David. God hates sin and loves forgiveness; in God-given repentance, King David despised his sinful inclinations and sought God's pardon throughout his life. David is a man after God's own heart because David, like God, hates sin and loves forgiveness.

Christ Jesus is proof that God hates sin and loves forgiveness. Jesus died on the cross to redeem you from sin. At the cross, God offered himself up for the forgiveness of your sins. The heart of God wants to remove your sins and give you his forgiveness.

Prayer starter: Lord Jesus, make me a man after your own heart. Teach me to hate sin and love your forgiveness . . .

THE GREATER ONE TO COME

The LORD says to my Lord: "Sit at my right hand, until I make your enemies your footstool."

Psalm 110:1

Parents prepare the way for the next generation by protecting their children. Teachers prepare the way for the next generation by imparting wisdom, both in and out of the classroom. Bosses ready the next generation of workers by allowing interns to plan a company event or critique the company website. The definition of maturity is preparing the way for your successors.

Resisting the growth of potential successors is a sign of immaturity. Jealous kings imprison the person next in line to the throne. Anxious bosses fire talented young managers. Fearful of being surpassed, insecure professors fail prodigy students.

David showed spiritual maturity by recognizing that a much greater King would one day occupy his throne. Being a prophet as well as a king, David paved the way for the coming Messiah by writing many prophetic psalms. David welcomed the coming of this greater King—our Lord Jesus.

Both Jesus and David recognized the important connection between them. As Jesus' conflict with the religious leaders of his day came to a head, the Lord asked the Pharisees this question: "What do you think about the Christ? Whose son is he?"

The Pharisees knew the answer: Messiah would be the son of David. Then, using David's own words, Jesus showed them how blind they were to their Messiah's identity and work:

ow is it then that David, in the Spirit, calls him Lord, aying, "The Lord said to my Lord, 'Sit at my right hand, ntil I put your enemies under your feet'"?

Matthew 22:43–44

avid recognized the coming Messiah as both his escendant ("son") and his God ("Lord"). Christ Jesus, e son of David, is King above all kings. He rules over all reation in perfect justice and mercy. Jesus forgives sins nd offers eternal life. There is no king like Jesus!

aturity means recognizing there is someone far greater, omeone far stronger and wiser than you are. Christ Jesus that greater one, the stronger, wiser one. By faith in him, ou become truly wise, truly strong—strong in the Lord.

Prayer starter: King of kings and Lord of lords, give me strength to recognize your far greater strength . . .

TURNING WORDS INTO ACTION

God is my strength and power.

2 Samuel 22:33 KJV

Talk is cheap. It costs nothing to promise . . .

- "I will turn my life around."
- "I will be a better husband, a better father for my family."
- "I will get it done."

These words cost nothing more than the breath it takes to say them.

Actions, on the other hand, are costly. It takes work, sweat, and sometimes blood to turn words into actions. Slivers, scrapes, and sleepless nights are the currency of action. Early mornings, late nights, and lots of energy are the price you pay to back up your promises.

For weeks now, we have been reading about David being strong in the Lord. David talked and wrote a lot about this lifestyle. And he lived it out. David was strong in the Lord, because the Lord gave him strength to turn his talk into action. Because the Holy Spirit was at work in David, David could walk the talk.

Our Lord claims to be mighty, merciful, and forgiving. He claims to see—and care about—the suffering of his people. He claims to be wise and good. And he backs up those words with actions. He walks the talk, as it were. In fact, Jesus Christ is the Word of God in action.

To rescue us from our sins, Jesus exchanged his glory as King of heaven for the humiliation of life as a human being here on earth.

e placed himself under the Law of God, keeping that
aw—the Law you could not keep—in your place. Then he
ied in agony on the cross that should have been yours,
sing to life again on the third day.

ealizing and believing that, you can turn from sin and
ollow your Savior. In Jesus, you can make promises and
eep them. In Jesus, your words and actions can be
igned. When you fail (and like David, you *will* fail), you
an run to your Redeemer for forgiveness.

tanding firm in that forgiveness, you are strong in the Lord.

Prayer starter: Holy Spirit, turn my words into actions. Make me truly strong, strong in the Lord and in your mighty power . . .

SUNDAY

Copper wire connects electricity from the power source to the electrical outlet. Similarly, faith connects you to Jesus. Scripture has plenty to say about faith:

Immediately the father of the child cried out and said, "I believe; help my unbelief!"

Mark 9:24

Through him we have also obtained access by faith into this grace in which we stand, and we rejoice in hope of the glory of God.

Romans 5:2

Therefore, since we are surrounded by so great a cloud of witnesses, let us also lay aside every weight, and sin which clings so closely, and let us run with endurance the race that is set before us.

Hebrews 12:1

Jesus Christ delivers his strength and power to you through the gift of faith. Faith in Christ connects you to the ultimate power source.

A NOTE FROM THE AUTHOR

Your family thinks of you as the strongest man in the world. People at work assume you can carry loads of responsibility. People at church think of you as a rock, a towering example of faith.

But you know the truth. You know that your silence often covers up your fears, that your firm resolve is sometimes just a front for anxiety. You know your weaknesses more deeply than any friend or colleague.

My prayer for you is that you will rely more and more fully on the Lord's strength, that you will learn to know him more completely in his Word, and that you would trust him more and more deeply. In short, I pray that you will be strong in the Lord.

He will never, ever fail!

A. Trevor Sutton

If this book has made a difference in your life or if you have simply enjoyed it, we would like to hear from you. Your words will encourage us! If you have suggestions for us to consider as we create books like this in the future, please send those, too.

Send e-mail to

editor@CTAinc.com and include the subject line: STL6SC

Write to

Editorial Manager, Department STL6SC, CTA, Inc. PO Box 1205, Fenton, MO 63026-1205

Or leave a product review at

www.CTAinc.com (search STL6SC).